Be an eco hero

At home

Sue Barraclough

SEA-TO-SEA
Mankato Collingwood London

This edition first published in 2013 by
Sea-to-Sea Publications
Distributed by Black Rabbit Books
P.O. Box 3263, Mankato, Minnesota
56002

Printed in the United States of
America, North Mankato, MN

9 8 7 6 5 4 3 2

Published by arrangement with the
Watts Publishing Group Ltd. London.

Library of Congress Cataloging-in-
Publication Data

Barraclough, Sue.
 Be an eco hero at home / Sue Barraclough.
   p. cm. -- (Be an eco hero)
 Includes index.
 ISBN 978-1-59771-379-5 (library binding)
 1. Environmentalism--Juvenile literature. I.
Title.
 GE195.5B37 2013
 640.286--dc23

                    2011049897

Series Editor: Sarah Peutrill
Art Director: Jonathan Hair
Design: Robert Walster,
Big Blu Design
Illustrator: Gary Swift

Credits: Anyka/istockphoto: 14bl.
Timur Arbaev/istockphoto: 14cr. Gerald
Barnard/istockphoto: 16r. Todd Bates/
Istockphoto: 23c. Martin Carlsson/
istockphoto: 11b. Tye Carnelli/istockphoto:
24b. Yvonne Chamberlain/istockphoto:
6t. Kimberley Deprey/istockphoto:
21t. Elena Elisseeva /Shutterstock:
19cl. Elnur/Shutterstock: 25l. EML/
Shutterstock: 10r. Mandy Godbehear/
istockphoto: 18b. Kim Gunkel/istockphoto:
13bl. Hallgerd/Shutterstock: 19b. Andrew
Hill/istockphoto: 15br. J Hindman/
Shutterstock: 16l. Justin Horrocks/
istockphoto: 13tc. Image Source/Corbis:
8t. istockphoto: 23b. Johanna Goodyear/
Dreamstime: 15bl. Andrey Kuzmin /
Shutterstock: 10l. Edyta Luiek/istockphoto:
19t. Mona Mekela/istockphoto: 25cl.
Jim Mills/istockphoto: 23t. Monkey
Business Images/Shutterstock: 19cr.
Juriah Mosin/Shutterstock: 6b, 13br.
Ramplett/istockphoto: front cover, 25cr.
RAT87/Shutterstock: 25b. Morley Read/
istockphoto: 9. runamock/istockphoto: 17.
Chris Fairclough/Franklin Watts: 13tl.
Jorge Salcedo/istockphoto: 14tr. Kristian
Sekulic /istockphoto: 8b. Nina Shannon/
istockphoto: 15t. sonyat/istockphoto:
22. Studio Araminta/Shutterstock: 25tr.
Tihis/Shutterstock: 13tr. Deniz Unlusu/
istockphoto: 18tl. Wishlist Images: 7, 20,
26, 27. Feng Yu/Shutterstock: 25tc. Sergey
Zavalnyuk/istockphoto: 21b.

RD/6000006415/001
May 2012

Contents

Find out ways to help your planet in this book and become an eco hero like me!

At Home   6

Using Energy   8

Why Save Energy?   10

Saving Energy   12

Using Water   14

Why Save Water?   16

Saving Water   18

Why Reduce, Reuse, Recycle?   20

Reducing Waste   22

Reuse and Recycle   24

Eco Hero Activities   26

Glossary   28

Learn More   29

Index   30

Words in **bold** are in the glossary on page 28.

At Home

Our homes are full of things that use **energy**. We use **gas** for cooking and for heating our homes. We use **electricity** for lights and to make machines work.

We use water in many ways around the home, too. We use it for baths, showers, toilets, and cleaning cars.

Think of all the things we have in our homes, from furniture to **packaging**, TVs to clothing. All these things are made using energy.

Energy and water are very important to us. Eco heroes don't waste them!

Using Energy

We all use a lot of energy, such as electricity, in our homes every day. Think of all the things we do that use electricity.

All around you there are many other homes using energy, too. So if we all save energy, it can make a big difference.

Why Save Energy?

Most energy is **generated** by burning **fossil fuels,** such as coal. Electricity is generated in **power plants** and travels along power lines like these to our homes.

Power transmission lines

Power plant

Homes

Fossil fuels will not last forever and we are using them up quickly. Burning fossil fuels also fills the air with dangerous gases.

You can be an eco hero by using less energy. For example, you can help to choose light bulbs that are energy **efficient**. This means they use less energy and last much longer.

11

Saving Energy

There are many easy ways to save energy.

Be an eco hero by:

- Wearing warm clothing and turning down heating to save energy.
- Turning off lights in empty rooms.
- Not leaving TVs, CD and DVD players, and other items on standby.
- Reading a book or playing a game instead of watching TV.
- Turning off and unplugging cell phone rechargers when not in use.

Unplug

Flip off

Turn off

Wear warm clothing

Read a book

Using Water

We all use a lot of water in our homes every day. Think about all the things you do every day that use water.

Washing hands

Drinking water

Flushing the toilet

Can you think of ways to use less water?

Brushing teeth

Boiling the kettle

Watering the garden

15

Why Save Water?

Water falls from the sky as rain. It is stored in lakes and **reservoirs**. It is cleaned and pumped along pipes to faucets in our homes. This takes energy.

Rainwater

Faucet

Clean, fresh water is **precious**. But, the number of people living on our planet is growing. We all have to share the supply of water. When there is not enough rain, some places can get **droughts**.

If we all save water, it can make a big difference. You can be an eco hero by saving water at home.

Saving Water

• Asking an adult to repair dripping faucets. A dripping faucet wastes more than a whole gallon of water every day.

• Using a bucket to wash the car, not a hose.

- Using a watering can, not a hose to water plants.

- Filling the dishwasher: one full load uses less water than several small loads.

- Not leaving the water running while you brush your teeth.

- Having a short shower instead of a bath.

Why Reduce, Reuse, Recycle?

Everything we buy and use is made using energy. Glass, plastic, paper, food, toys, clothing, books, and machines are all made using energy and **raw materials**.

Factories use energy and make pollution.

Reducing waste, **reusing,** and **recycling** means:
- less energy and raw materials are used
- less **pollution**
- less garbage going to **landfill sites.**

Our landfill sites are almost full.

Reducing Waste

Reducing waste means shopping carefully so you have less garbage to throw away at home.

Be an eco hero by:

• Choosing things with less packaging.

Buy loose fruit and vegetables.

Refill bottles.

• Choosing to use refillable drinks bottles.

• Taking your own bags to the grocery store.

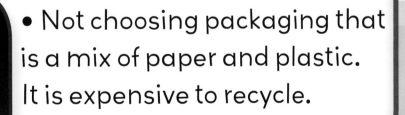

Reuse bags.

• Choosing packaging, such as glass or paper, that can be recycled easily.

• Not choosing packaging that is a mix of paper and plastic. It is expensive to recycle.

Avoid cartons if you can.

Reuse and Recycle

You can also save energy by reusing things and recycling. Reusing something makes the most of the time, energy, materials, and money used to make it. Reusing and recycling cuts down pollution and often saves water, too.

Be an eco hero and reuse things:

- Repair and repaint before you replace.
- Donate old toys and clothing to Goodwill Stores.
- Choose reusables not **disposables.**

Make donations.

Be an eco hero by recycling. All these things can be recycled.

Metal cans

Glass bottles and jars

Some plastics

Food waste

Paper and cardboard

Eco Hero Activities

Here are some ideas that will make your home fit for an eco hero:

Stop the drafts! Reuse some old socks to make a draft stopper like this. Ask an adult to help you.

Stuff old socks with shredded newspaper.

How do the temperatures differ in your house? Which rooms and walls are cooler and which are warmer? Use a thermometer to find out. You could put draft stoppers in the coldest rooms.

Get smart! Think of ways to reuse things. You could turn cereal boxes into magazine racks by covering them in used gift wrap.

Glossary

disposable   An item that is made to be thrown away after it is used.

drought   A long period of time when there is very little or no rain.

efficient   Something that works quickly and well.

electricity   Form of energy that makes heat or light that can also be used to make machines work.

energy   Something that makes things work, move, or change.

fossil fuel   Materials found deep under the ground and formed over millions of years from dead animals and plants.

fuel   Material used to make heat or light, usually by being burned. Coal, gas, and oil are types of fuel.

gas   Airlike substance that you cannot see.

generate   To produce energy in a certain form.

landfill site   A huge hole in the ground where garbage is buried.

packaging   Bottles, packages, and boxes used to keep food and other products safe and fresh.

pollution   Substance that dirties or poisons air, earth, or water.

power plant   A factory that generates electricity.

precious   Something that has great value because it is rare, expensive, or important.

raw material   Substance such as wood or oil that is used to make things.

recycling   Using materials again or making them into something new.

reservoir   A large lake used to store water.

reusing   Using something again.

Learn More

This book shows you some of the ways you can be an eco hero. But there is plenty more you can do to save the planet. Here are some web sites that have ideas and information to help you learn more about being an eco hero:

www.planetpals.com/

Over 300 pages of activities, lesson plans, facts, fun, including Earthzone, where you can take quizzes, color, play, or make something today.

www.ecokids.ca/pub/eco_info/topics/water/ water/index.cfm
Read the Story of Water and find out why it is important to save it.

www.childrenoftheearth.org/index.htm
Web site with recycling news, tips, and much more.

www.eia.gov/kids/energy
Find out all about global warming and the things we can all do to tackle it from the U.S. Energy Information Administration's web site.

Note to parents and teachers: Every effort has been made by the Publishers to ensure that these web sites are suitable for children, that they are of the highest educational value, and that they contain no inappropriate or offensive material. However, because of the nature of the Internet, it is impossible to guarantee that the contents of these sites will not be altered. We strongly advise that Internet access is supervised by a responsible adult.

Index

metal 25

disposables 24, 28

droughts 17, 28

electricity 6, 8, 10, 28

energy 6, 7, 8, 9, 10, 16, 20, 21, 24, 28

food 20, 25, 28

fossil fuels 10, 11, 28

garbage 21, 22

glass 20, 23, 25

heating 6, 12

landfill sites 21, 28

packaging 7, 22, 23, 28

paper 20, 23, 25

plastic 20, 23, 25

pollution 21, 24, 28

power plants 10, 28

raw materials 20, 21, 24, 28

recycle 20, 21, 23, 24, 25, 28, 29

reducing waste 20, 21, 22, 23

reuse 20, 21, 24, 25, 26, 27

saving energy 9, 10, 11, 12, 13, 29

saving water 14, 16, 17, 18, 19, 29

water 6, 7, 14, 15, 16, 17, 24, 29